THE OFFICIAL

ANNUAL 2022

Designed by **Daniel May**

A Grange Publication

© 2021. Published by Grange Communications Ltd., Edinburgh, under licence from The Liverpool Football Club. Printed in the EU.

ISBN: 978-1-913578-76-3

CONTENTS

LFC HONOURS BOARD

ENGLISH LEAGUE CHAMPIONS
1900/01, 1905/06, 1921/22, 1922/23, 1946/47, 1963/64, 1965/66, 1972/73, 1975/76, 1976/77, 1978/79, 1979/80, 1981/82, 1982/83, 1983/84, 1985/86, 1987/88, 1989/90, 2019/20

FA CUP WINNERS
1965, 1974, 1986, 1989, 1992, 2001, 2006

LEAGUE CUP WINNERS
1981, 1982, 1983, 1984, 1995, 2001, 2003, 2012

EUROPEAN CUP/ CHAMPIONS LEAGUE WINNERS
1977, 1978, 1981, 1984, 2005, 2019

UEFA CUP WINNERS
1973, 1976, 2001

FIFA CLUB WORLD CUP WINNERS
2019

UEFA SUPER CUP WINNERS
1977, 2001, 2005, 2019

SECOND DIVISION CHAMPIONS
1893/94, 1895/96, 1904/05, 1961/62

FA YOUTH CUP WINNERS
1995/96, 2005/06, 2006/07, 2018/19

FOOTBALL LEAGUE SUPER CUP WINNERS
1985/86

WOMEN'S SUPER LEAGUE CHAMPIONS
2013, 2014

CHARITY/COMMUNITY SHIELD WINNERS
1964*, 1965*, 1966, 1974, 1976, 1977*, 1979, 1980, 1982, 1986*, 1988, 1989, 1990*, 2001, 2006 (*shared)

RESERVE LEAGUE CHAMPIONS
1955/56, 1968/69, 1969/70, 1970/71, 1972/73, 1973/74, 1974/75, 1975/76, 1976/77, 1978/79, 1979/80, 1980/81, 1981/82, 1983/84, 1984/85, 1989/90, 1999/2000, 2007/08

2020/21 SEASON REVIEW

The 2020/21 football season may not be one we recall with much affection in years to come. An unprecedented injury crisis, ongoing confusion and controversy surrounding VAR, plus the continued absence of supporters in stadiums made for a difficult season for Liverpool's squad who were trying to defend their Premier League title, not to mention facing serious challenges for other honours. However, the Reds never gave up, fought on and come the final day, at least there were smiles back on faces as we achieved a brilliant Top 4 finish.

AUGUST & SEPTEMBER

Just like the season before, Liverpool's campaign began with a penalty shoot-out defeat in the Community Shield at Wembley. Nevertheless, optimism remained high and, when the real business got underway a fortnight later, Mo Salah was the hat-trick hero as newly-promoted Leeds were beaten in a seven-goal thriller. A further boost came with the high-profile signings of Thiago Alcântara and Diogo Jota, who both made impressive starts to their Liverpool careers as the champions went on to register four wins out of four in September.

🏁 RESULTS

August

29	Arsenal (n)	CS	1-1 (4-5 on pens)

*played at Wembley

September

12	Leeds United (h)	PL	4-3
20	Chelsea (a)	PL	2-0
24	Lincoln City (a)	CC	7-2
28	Arsenal (h)	PL	3-1

OCTOBER

We were not to know it at the time, but this was to prove the pivotal month in Liverpool's season. Although elimination from the Carabao Cup was followed by a defeat at Villa Park that sent shockwaves reverberating through the game, much more damaging was an incident in the 11th minute of the Merseyside derby. Virgil van Dijk was stretchered off following a collision with Jordan Pickford and subsequently ruled out for the remainder of the campaign. The Reds responded positively to record four straight victories post-Everton, but the loss of van Dijk was one that Liverpool would never truly recover from.

🔊 RESULTS

01	Arsenal (h)	CC	0-0 (4-5 on pens)
04	Aston Villa (a)	PL	2-7
17	Everton (a)	PL	2-2
21	Ajax (a)	CL	1-0
24	Sheffield United (h)	PL	2-1
27	FC Midtjylland (h)	CL	2-0
31	West Ham United (h)	PL	2-1

NOVEMBER

There was more bad news on the injury front in November, when Joe Gomez also had his season prematurely curtailed. It meant Liverpool's ranks were now severely depleted in the centre of defence, but the champions somehow maintained their unbeaten start in the Premier League and broke the club's longest unbeaten league run at Anfield in the process. However, when a first Champions League defeat at home to Atalanta – a team they had emphatically beaten at the start of the month – was swiftly followed by a disappointing draw away to Brighton, the warning signs began to flicker.

🔊 RESULTS

03	Atalanta (a)	CL	5-0
08	Manchester City (a)	PL	1-1
21	Leicester City (h)	PL	3-0
25	Atalanta (h)	CL	0-2
28	Brighton & Hove Albion (a)	PL	1-1

DECEMBER

With qualification from the Champions League group phase safely assured with a game to spare, Liverpool finally welcomed fans back to Anfield in December. The lucky 2,000 that were allowed in witnessed what was to be the biggest home win of the season against Wolves. The team's best performance of the campaign, though, undoubtedly came at Crystal Palace. Just days after Roberto Firmino's last-minute goal secured a vital three points at home to Spurs, the reigning champions turned on the style to register a thumping seven-goal victory - their biggest in the Premier League and one that kept them top of the tree at Christmas.

RESULTS

01	Ajax (h)	CL	1-0
06	Wolverhampton Wanderers (h)	PL	4-0
09	FC Midtjylland (a)	CL	1-1
13	Fulham (a)	PL	1-1
16	Tottenham Hotspur (h)	PL	2-1
19	Crystal Palace (a)	PL	7-0
27	West Bromwich Albion (h)	PL	1-1
31	Newcastle United (a)	PL	0-0

JANUARY

This was the month when Liverpool's season really began to unravel. A bad start to 2021 saw the Reds not only surrender top spot in the Premier League but also their long-unbeaten home record. Burnley were the surprise first winners at Anfield in over three years and, to cap a miserable few days, interest in the FA Cup was then brought to a halt with a fourth round defeat at Old Trafford. The month concluded with impressive back-to-back victories in London, but these were tempered by another season-ending injury to a centre-back, this time Joël Matip, prompting the emergency loan signings of Ozan Kabak and Ben Davies.

RESULTS

04	Southampton (a)	PL	0-1
08	Aston Villa (a)	FA	4-1
17	Manchester United (h)	PL	0-0
21	Burnley (h)	PL	0-1
24	Manchester United (a)	FA	2-3
28	Tottenham Hotspur (a)	PL	3-1
31	West Ham United (a)	PL	3-1

FEBRUARY

Amidst a defensive injury crisis, the likes of which would have severely tested the resolve of any club, Liverpool's fortunes stumbled from bad to worse during the first two weeks of February. Three successive defeats, including two at home, saw them sink further down the table and extinguished any aspirations of a successful title defence. To compound the misery, Everton then won at Anfield for the first time since 1999 and, rubbing further salt into the wound, captain Jordan Henderson limped off to join the ever-increasing long-term injury list.

RESULTS

03	Brighton & Hove Albion (h)	PL	0-1
07	Manchester City (h)	PL	1-4
13	Leicester City (a)	PL	1-3
16	RB Leipzig (a) *played in Budapest	CL	2-0
20	Everton (h)	PL	0-2
28	Sheffield United (a)	PL	2-0

MARCH

The once impregnable 'fortress Anfield' now seemed to be crumbling as Chelsea and Fulham became the latest teams to depart L4 with maximum points. Solace came in the Champions League where a place in the quarter-final was comfortably secured, but the prospect of qualifying for the following season's tournament was looking less and less likely. With ten Premier League games remaining Liverpool found themselves in 8th place, seven points adrift of the top four. Wolves away was a must-win and on his first return to Molineux in a red shirt, Diogo Jota duly delivered.

RESULTS

04	Chelsea (h)	PL	0-1
07	Fulham (h)	PL	0-1
10	RB Leipzig (h) *played in Budapest	CL	2-0
15	Wolverhampton Wanderers (a)	PL	1-0

APRIL

It was a case of roles reversed in April. Unable to overturn a first leg deficit suffered in Spain, Liverpool exited the Champions League, but domestically embarked on an unbeaten run in a bid to save their season. Jota came off the bench to inspire the club's biggest top-flight away win over Arsenal, while Trent Alexander-Arnold curled in a stoppage-time winner to register the Reds' first home victory of the calendar year. Sadly, though, two late lapses of concentration saw crucial points dropped in successive games at the end of the month to raise doubts once again about whether Liverpool could achieve that much-needed top four finish.

RESULTS

03	Arsenal (a)	PL	3-0
06	Real Madrid (a)	CL	1-3
10	Aston Villa (h)	PL	2-1
14	Real Madrid (h)	CL	0-0
19	Leeds United (a)	PL	1-1
24	Newcastle United (h)	PL	1-1

MAY

To be in with a chance of securing Champions League qualification the task was clear; Liverpool had to win all five of their remaining Premier League games. It was as simple as that. Thankfully, May was the month in which Jürgen Klopp's team finally rediscovered their true form. Thiago netted his first goal for the Reds, Manchester United were comprehensively beaten at Old Trafford, Alisson made history away to West Brom (see pages 24-25) and Nathaniel Phillips grew in stature with every game. It set up a final-day clash at home to Crystal Palace when 10,000 fans were able to see the Reds achieve what many had deemed impossible just a few weeks previous. Despite all the trials and tribulations of what had been a testing nine months it was, with a huge sigh of relief, a case of mission accomplished.

RESULTS

08	Southampton (h)	PL	2-0
13	Manchester United (a)	PL	4-2
16	West Bromwich Albion (a)	PL	2-1
19	Burnley (a)	PL	3-0
23	Crystal Palace (h)	PL	2-0

FINAL LEAGUE TABLE

			P	W	D	L	F	A	GD	PTS
1		Manchester City	38	27	5	6	83	32	51	86
2		Manchester United	38	21	11	6	73	44	29	74
3		Liverpool	38	20	9	9	68	42	26	69
4		Chelsea	38	19	10	9	58	36	22	67
5		Leicester City	38	20	6	12	68	50	18	66
6		West Ham United	38	19	8	11	62	47	15	65
7		Tottenham Hotspur	38	18	8	12	68	45	23	62
8		Arsenal	38	18	7	13	55	39	16	61
9		Leeds United	38	18	5	15	62	54	8	59
10		Everton	38	17	8	13	47	48	-1	59
11		Aston Villa	38	16	7	15	55	46	9	55
12		Newcastle United	38	12	9	17	46	62	-16	45
13		Wolverhampton Wanderers	38	12	9	17	36	52	-16	45
14		Crystal Palace	38	12	8	18	41	66	-25	44
15		Southampton	38	12	7	19	47	68	-21	43
16		Brighton and Hove Albion	38	9	14	15	40	46	-6	41
17		Burnley	38	10	9	19	33	55	-22	39
18		Fulham	38	5	13	20	27	53	-26	28
19		West Bromwich Albion	38	5	11	22	35	76	-41	26
20		Sheffield United	38	7	2	29	20	63	-43	23

"This is big. If someone had told me five or six weeks ago that we would finish the season in third, I would have said it was impossible. It was absolutely out of reach. But the good thing this year is how we responded when we didn't feel good because too many things happened to us."

Jürgen Klopp

"We went through a lot this season. The empty stadiums, coupled with the great hurdles we have faced, would have shattered any other team. Not us. We came third. And never stopped believing."

Mo Salah

"Thank God, we have a team who are really positive. Not playing in the Champions League next season would have been a big blow. We can now look at it in the respect that we have won the Champions League, then the Premier League and will be playing in the Champions League again despite a difficult season, which I think is good."

Sadio Mané

INSIDE THE
AXA TRAINING CENTRE

Take an exclusive peek behind the gates of Liverpool's stunning new ultra-modern training base in Kirkby...

More than two years of construction work has created a world-class facility for Jürgen Klopp and his squad, who moved there from Melwood during the 2020/21 season.

The complex, which has a base measurement of 9,200sqm, is on the same site as the club's Academy and is about a 15-minute drive from the old training ground in West Derby.

Liverpool Sporting Director Michael Edwards:

"Since I have been at Liverpool there has been a desire for us to all be on the same site. To be honest, I think many people before me wanted the same thing and now we have been lucky enough to deliver that.

"The other key reason was to make sure that we were giving our players and staff up-to-date, world-class facilities.

"Melwood was such an iconic place, with some great memories for all those people that have worked there; hopefully Kirkby will become the same."

Some stand-out features of the new AXA Training Centre...

- ✓ Three pristine full-size pitches

- ✓ A dedicated goalkeeping space

- ✓ Two head-tennis areas

- ✓ A 30x30m Astroturf pitch for smaller ball exercises

- ✓ A state-of-the-art gym, featuring floor-to-ceiling glass views out onto the training pitches

- ✓ Rehabilitation areas

- ✓ An altitude room to aid fitness

- ✓ A hydrotherapy area including a swimming pool and hot and cold pools for recovery

- ✓ Designated presentation spaces for team meetings and video analysis

- ✓ A world-class kitchen to meet the nutritional needs of professional athletes

- ✓ Walls adorned with imagery acknowledging and celebrating the club's illustrious history

- ✓ A Champions Walk proudly listing all Liverpool's honours

Managers' Gallery

A CHAMPIONS WALK PROUDLY LISTING ALL LIVERPOOL'S HONOURS

MIGHTY MO'S TOP 10 MAGICAL MOMENTS

Mohamed Salah has been smashing goalscoring records for fun since signing for Liverpool in the summer of 2017. In the process he's also collected more than his fair share of honours. The 'Egyptian King's' legendary status at the club is already assured and hopefully our number 11 has many more amazing years ahead of him in a red shirt. But what's your favourite Mo memory? Here's ten to get you thinking…

SPOT ON FOR CHAMPIONS LEAGUE GLORY
Madrid, 1 June 2019

He's scored better goals but has there been a more important one? Just two minutes into the biggest game of his life he stepped up to the penalty spot and held his nerve amid nail-biting tension to give Liverpool a crucial early lead in the Champions League final against Tottenham.

AND NOW YOU'RE GONNA BELIEVE US…
Anfield, 19 January 2020

This was the moment when Kopites finally allowed themselves to believe the 30-year wait for a league title was almost over. Racing onto an Alisson goal-kick, Salah's perfect first touch, blistering pace and clinical finish sealed a famous victory at home to Manchester United.

GOLDEN BOOTS
2017/18

In terms of goalscoring, no player has enjoyed a better debut season at Anfield than Salah, who netted an incredible 44 times in all competitions. 32 of those came in the Premier League, setting a new record for a 38-game season and securing him the coveted Golden Boot award.

WINNING THE PUSKAS
Anfield, 10 December 2017

Salah treated us to so many great goals during his first season in a red shirt that debate will forever rage as to what was his best. But this strike, his first-ever derby goal, was deemed good enough to win the prestigious FIFA 'Puskas' Goal of the Year award.

TRIPLE PLAYER OF THE YEAR
May 2018

Although Salah's first season at Liverpool ended with no silverware for the team, it was a campaign of personal glory; his exceptional form being recognised with a trio of Player of the Year prizes from the PFA, Football Writers and Premier League.

FOUR-MIDABLE V THE HORNETS
Anfield, 17 March 2018

Mo's first hat-trick for the club came in his 41st game but it was well worth the wait because he then went one better and added a fourth! On a wintry evening at Anfield, it was Watford who found themselves on the receiving end of this masterclass in finishing.

ARRIVEDERCI ROMA
Anfield, 24 April 2018

Salah stole the headlines and set Liverpool on course for a place in the Champions League final with a memorable brace against his former club. Less than 12 months after leaving Roma, he broke their hearts again by firing the Reds into a decisive 2-0 half-time lead.

SILENCING CITY
Etihad Stadium, 10 April 2018

Any hopes Manchester City may have harboured of overturning the first-leg deficit in this Champions League quarter-final tie evaporated the moment Salah rounded off a swift counter-attack by deftly dinking the ball home from a tight angle in front of the ecstatic travelling Liverpudlians.

CHELSEA NET-BUSTER
Anfield, 14 April 2019

Arguably Mo's best strike in a red shirt, he cut in from the right wing and unleashed an unstoppable rocket of a shot with his left foot from 30-yards out. It whizzed past the despairing dive of the keeper and almost burst the Kop net.

THE SCOURGE OF UNITED ONCE AGAIN
Old Trafford, 13 May 2021

With the hosts threatening a comeback that would have derailed Liverpool's bid for Champions League qualification, Salah took centre stage with a display of ice-cool composure in the dying minutes. A sudden breakaway sent him racing through on goal and he calmly finished to seal an impressive win.

1

ALISSON **BECKER**

1

GOALKEEPER

66

TRENT

ALEXANDER-ARNOLD

DEFENDER

WHEN KLOPP MET THE KIDS

Here's what happened when Jürgen Klopp agreed to be quizzed by members of the Liverpool under-8s squad (now under-9s)...

When you were young, what did your coach tell you to do when you played football?

My coach was actually the mailman from my home village, so he worked the whole day and only came once a week for training. But he told us, "Play as much football as you can." And that's what we did.

What has been your best day in football so far?

I had a few really good ones. As a player I once scored four goals in a game; that was for sure the best day of my playing time. As a manager it's not that easy. We got promoted with Mainz in Germany, became champions with Dortmund, won the double with Dortmund. About the Liverpool things you know, but without winning something, just for a game I would say the best moment is...the Barcelona home game. "Corner taken quickly." Eh? That was for sure one of the best moments ever.

Who's your all-time favourite player and why?

My favourite player - you don't know him, unfortunately - it's Karlheinz Förster. He was a centre-half at my favourite club [Vfb Stuttgart]. The No. 4 was my favourite player and when I started playing professional football we always got the number on our back randomly, a little bit based on position, but then during my career we got the opportunity to choose a fixed number, and even when I was a striker at that time, I took the No. 4, because of Karlheinz Förster. Coincidentally or not, a little bit later I was a defender!

What is your favourite English restaurant and why?

Can I be honest here?! I'm not 100% sure about the English food still. When you are from Germany you are just used to other things, but fish and chips I love. Black pudding...I tried at least.

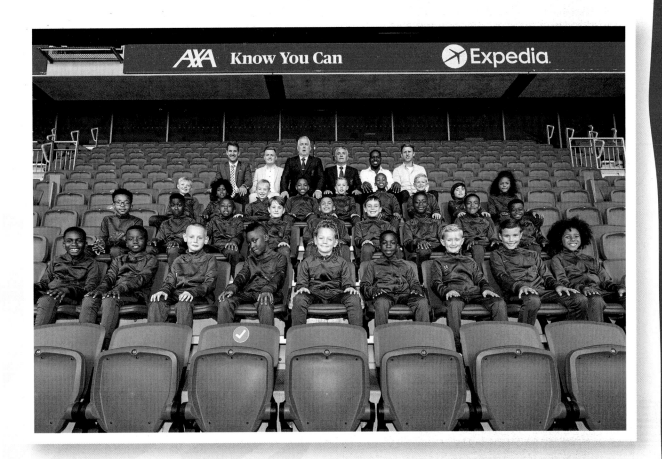

"Train, train, train - as much as you can. Try to learn as much as you can, become the best version of yourself, the best player you can be. Whatever that means in the end" – Jürgen Klopp

It's great to see so many pre-Academy players, such as Trent and Curtis, playing for the first team. What advice could you give me to help me one day achieve this?

Train, train, train - as much as you can. Try to learn as much as you can, become the best version of yourself, the best player you can be. Whatever that means in the end. Some other people, like me, make those decisions. Enjoy football - very important - play as much as you can, because most of the things you will not learn in training, you learn by doing them wherever it is, if you play with your friends, somewhere in the park, or with your friends, on the training ground, that's where you learn the most.

> ## "Be confident, stay confident, because there's no reason for not being confident" – Jürgen Klopp

What do you do when young players lose their confidence?

Confidence I think is based on positivity, that means if you're experienced yourself... You know as well, if you score a goal in a game, you just think, "Next time I'm in a similar situation, I will score again." Yeah. That's what confidence is, so if you didn't score the last time, it might feel different. What I try to do in these moments, I try to remind the boys of their real quality. So, be confident, stay confident, because there's no reason for not being confident.

Trent and Robbo are my favourite players, I watched their TV programme and they said you dance like a dad. Who do you think is a better dancer - Trent or Robbo?

Look, first of all, they are right. I had a few moments since I've been here where I had a reason to dance. I need reasons to dance, if we celebrate something, I would not start dancing now probably. Who is a better dancer? I think they are both not really skilled, both a bit stiff. They both stand in the corner and watch the others, and

laugh at the others who try to dance. But I think it's a good choice for your favourite players.

What made you come to Liverpool?

You were two years old when I joined Liverpool. Before that I trained another club, that was Borussia Dortmund. That's the team with the yellow shirts in Germany. Really good team. And then Liverpool called. And when you think a little about Liverpool you think about the wonderful stadium, the big success in the past, the great players who were here. So I fancied it a lot, and now it's already five years that I've been here.

Have you ever had a pan of Scouse, and if so, do you like it?

Yeah, I had it. Great, love it. In the beginning I was asked about English food, was not that happy, but Scouse is outstanding. But maybe it's not English food, it's Liverpool food, I think. So maybe that's why I like it.

Do you ever get mad in the dressing room when the game hasn't gone to plan?

Possibly, but usually I try, if we lost the game, it makes sense that you go home and maybe sleep a night before you then properly talk about it. You will realise that when you get older, in a lot of situations in your life it really makes sense that, if you feel anger, you just step aside or go home and sleep a night or think a little bit, and THEN you talk about it. Because then the emotions are out and you can speak about the things that really matter.

What preparation do you ask your players to do before a game?

We either way go to the hotel in the city where we play, by plane, train or bus, or we go to our hotel in Liverpool, and in the stadium the boys have their individual things. Some of them wear their own headphones, hear their own music, others hear the music which we have there for all the guys. But it's very calm, you hear the music but apart from that there's not a lot of talk. Then the boys get proper warmed up, with finishing and all these kinds of things.

After that we go in, the boys change again, out of their warm-up gear, that's now full of sweat, so change it, into the proper playing gear. And then it gets louder, then everybody is, like, active. James Milner, Hendo, all the guys are then really talking: "Come on, make

yourself ready"- these kinds of things. "Be ready, we want to win the game." After that we go out and try to win the game.

Who's the funniest player in the team?

Andy Robertson. That's easy. Thank you very much, a good question, easy answer. Andy Robertson.

What's your favourite Scouse saying?

'Sound.' So in the beginning, I didn't understand it at all, when somebody is like: "How are you?" "Sound." "How is this?" "Sound." I thought, 'sound'? So, yes, 'sound' is my favourite saying in Scouse.

Which outfield player would you put in goal if both goalkeepers got injured in a match?

First and foremost, I hope that never will happen! Probably then James Milner. Actually Millie played in pretty much every position for me, apart from goalkeeper, so, yeah. And if it doesn't work, we at least had fun! Because Millie was in goal. So, yeah, probably James.

2 6

ANDREW

ROBERTSON

X

DEFENDER

LIVERPOOL
FOOTBALL CLUB
YOU'LL NEVER WALK ALONE
EST·1892

4

VIRGIL VAN DIJK

DEFENDER

23

DIVINE INTERVENTION BY THE GOALSCORING GOALIE

In the long and illustrious history of Liverpool Football Club there has never been a moment like that which occurred in the 95th minute at The Hawthorns on Sunday 16 May 2021.

With Reds being held to a 1-1 draw by West Bromwich Albion, their aspirations of Champions League qualification were fading fast.

Nothing but a win would suffice. Deep into injury time, in what was surely the last attack, Sadio Mané forced a corner. Ninety-five minutes were showing on the clock. Time all but up.

It was a case of now or never as the red shirts packed into the box. There was a black shirt too. It belonged to Liverpool number one Alisson Becker.

Desperate times call for desperate measures, but not much hope was being pinned on Alisson's presence in the opposition penalty area.

A quick glance at the record books would tell you that in the previous 129 years of the club's existence, a competitive goal had never been registered in the name of a goalkeeper.

Of course, there's always a first time for everything and thankfully this was that moment…

Trent Alexander-Arnold whipped in the corner from the left and while Albion's defenders concentrated on staying close to those in red, they fatefully left the man in black unattended.

Just when you thought you had seen it all as a Liverpool supporter, Alisson rose to meet the ball with his head, connected with it sweetly and glanced it into the far corner. Cue disbelief and delirium.

> **"I TRIED TO LOOK AT THE BENCH BUT NOBODY CALLED ME AND THEN JOHNNY, JOHNNY ACHTEBERG CALLED ME WITH CONVICTION. AND THEN IT WAS THE PERFECT TIME, THE CROSS WAS BRILLIANT AGAIN AND I JUST TRIED TO PUT MY HEAD ON THE BALL AND I THINK IT WAS ONE OF THE BEST GOALS I SAW! IT IS THE BEST I HAVE SCORED…THIS IS THE ONLY ONE I'VE SCORED! I'M REALLY HAPPY."**
>
> Alisson

> **"I LOOKED AT MY WATCH, 94, AND I THOUGHT IT WAS GOING TO BE THE LAST KICK OF THE GAME. WE NEEDED TO WIN, SO I SHOUTED, 'GET UP IN THE BOX!' TO HIM! WE HAD NOTHING TO LOSE AND WE NEEDED TO PUT EVERYTHING INTO THE BOX WE HAD."**
>
> John Achteberg (goalkeeper coach)

TOP 10

It'll come as no surprise that Alisson's incredible goal topped Liverpool's 2020/21 Goal of the Season poll. For the record, here's the list in full as voted for by supporters on the club's official website…

1. **Alisson Becker** v West Bromwich Albion (a)
2. **Mohamed Salah** v Leeds United (h)
3. **Mohamed Salah** v West Ham United (a)
4. **Mohamed Salah** v Crystal Palace (a)
5. **Mohamed Salah** v Atalanta BC (a)
6. **Mohamed Salah** v Everton (a)
7. **Trent Alexander-Arnold** v Aston Villa (h)
8. **Mohamed Salah** v Leicester City (a)
9. **Rinsola Babajide** v Sheffield United Women (h)
10. **Mateusz Musialowski** v Newcastle United u18s (a)

> "I'VE NEVER SEEN ANYTHING LIKE THAT - GOOD TECHNIQUE, I WASN'T SURE WHAT I WAS SEEING. MY PART OF THE GOAL IS I DIDN'T SHOUT TO STAY BACK! HE WENT THERE AND WHAT A GOAL, IT'S INCREDIBLE."
>
> Jürgen Klopp

History had been made and there was barely time to restart the game. Jürgen Klopp's team remained on course for a top four finish but, understandably, all the post-match talk centred around the amazing achievement of Liverpool's first ever goalscoring goalkeeper. Our hero Ali!

SUPER SIX

In heading home Liverpool's sensational winner at West Brom, Alisson joined an elite group of just six goalkeepers to have scored in the Premier League, although none were more spectacular…

» **Peter Schmeichel**
for Aston Villa v Everton, October 2001

» **Brad Friedel**
for Blackburn v Charlton Athletic, February 2004

» **Paul Robinson**
for Tottenham Hotspur v Watford, March 2007

» **Tim Howard**
for Everton v Bolton Wanderers, January 2012

» **Asmir Begović**
for Stoke City v Southampton, November 2013

L.F.C. Foundation
THE CLUB'S OFFICIAL CHARITY

We are the LFC Foundation, the official charity of Liverpool Football Club. Our mission is to create life-changing opportunities for children, young people and families.

We do lots of impactful work in the community for both children and adults across the Liverpool City Region and beyond.

You will see us in your local sport centres, parks and in primary and secondary schools, providing a wide variety of programmes and engaging with people every day.

Here is just a snapshot of some of our programmes aimed at children and young people…

We offer lots of football opportunities through programmes such as Premier League Kicks, Player Development Programme and Mini Players.

We are passionate about getting young people active and trying new activities, which is why we have our GO PLAY! multi-sport programme and Game On, which allow children to benefit from a range of sports such as tennis and basketball.

Our #iWill programme encourages young people to come together and use their voice to tackle issues they feel passionate about and create positive changes in their community.

Our Premier League Primary Stars programme helps to inspire children to learn, be active and develop important life skills.

We work closely with LFC and club mascot, Mighty Red, to provide even more exciting opportunities for our local communities.

For more information about everything the LFC Foundation offers, visit our website:

liverpoolfc

WORDSEARCH

Around the world with the Reds…

Listed below are 21 worldwide destinations where Liverpool have competed in a major cup final. Can you find them in this grid by searching horizontally, vertically and diagonally?

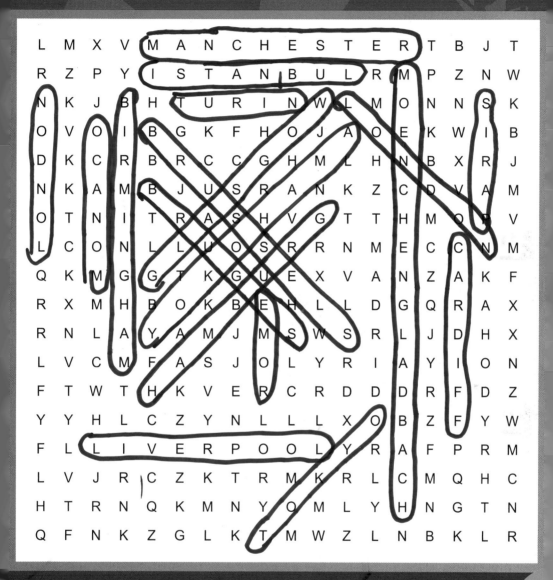

```
L M X V M A N C H E S T E R T B J T
R Z P Y I S T A N B U L R M P Z N W
N K J B H T U R I N W L M O N N S K
O V O I B G K F H O J A O E K W I B
D K C R B R C C G H M L H N B X R J
N K A M B J U S R A N K Z C D V A M
O T N I T R A S H V G T T H M O R V
L C O N L L U O S R R N M E C C N M
Q K M G G T K G U E X V A N Z A K F
R X M H B O K B E H L L D G Q R A X
R N L A Y A M J M S W S R L J D H X
L V C M F A S J O L Y R I A Y I O N
F T W T H K V E R C R D D D R F D Z
Y Y H L C Z Y N L L L X O B Z F Y W
F L L I V E R P O O L Y R A F P R M
L V J R C Z K T R M K R L C M Q H C
H T R N Q K M N Y O M L Y H N G T N
Q F N K Z G L K T M W Z L N B K L R
```

☑ London	☑ Manchester	☑ Cardiff
☑ Glasgow	☑ London	☑ Monaco
☑ Liverpool	☑ Birmingham	☑ Istanbul
☑ Moenchengladbach	☑ Paris	☑ Yokohama
☑ Bruges	☑ Tokyo	☐ Basel
☑ Rome	☑ Turin	☐ Madrid
☑ Hamburg	☑ Brussels	☐ Doha

*Test the memory of your parents or grandparents by seeing if they can remember in what year and in what competition these finals took place.

PS: For some destinations there is more than one answer!

IBRAHIMA **KONATÉ**

5

DEFENDER

JAMES **MILNER**

7

MIDFIELDER

THIAGO
Alcântara

The Beatles, tattoos, pizza and football; our Spanish midfielder
Thiago Alcântara discusses it all in this revealing interview…

What's the favourite place you've visited in Liverpool?

Before the COVID situation I tried to walk around the city. I went on the docks, and Anfield, the surroundings of the stadium - there was an amazing atmosphere there, what I feel before a game will be awesome. Yeah, it's an amazing city, very similar to my hometown, so I'm looking forward to ending this situation we're living in now so I can enjoy the city.

If you weren't a footballer what would you be?

Anything related to sport, because my dad was a football player, my mum was a volleyball player, so it was an easy choice to be involved in sport.

If you had to pick either Steven Gerrard or Xabi Alonso to partner you in midfield, who would it be and why?

Wow. Well, the midfield is so big, I can pick both. We can play with three midfielders. They were legends here at this club, they were legends in football. I have massive respect for the story of Steven Gerrard in this club, he changed the club as well. I'm looking forward to meeting him. And with Xabi, Xabi was a friend, a teammate and a teacher for me while we were playing together for Bayern and the national team, I like him a lot and respect him as a player, as a person and now as a coach. They were machines, they were amazing football players.

Who was your inspiration growing up?

Definitely my father. He was a football player, and he was my mirror in that time. For me, it was not so important what I saw on the pitch, but I had the luck to see the behaviour of a football player off the pitch. How many hours he sleeps, how he has to eat - so it was a kind of example for me.

What were your thoughts after playing against Liverpool in the Champions League for Bayern Munich?

We were facing a great team and in all the areas they were strong: defending, attacking. But, yeah, when we got in the stadium it was amazing, before the game to hear the chants, and also to hear the Champions League anthem, you just get motivated for the game, it amazing feeling.

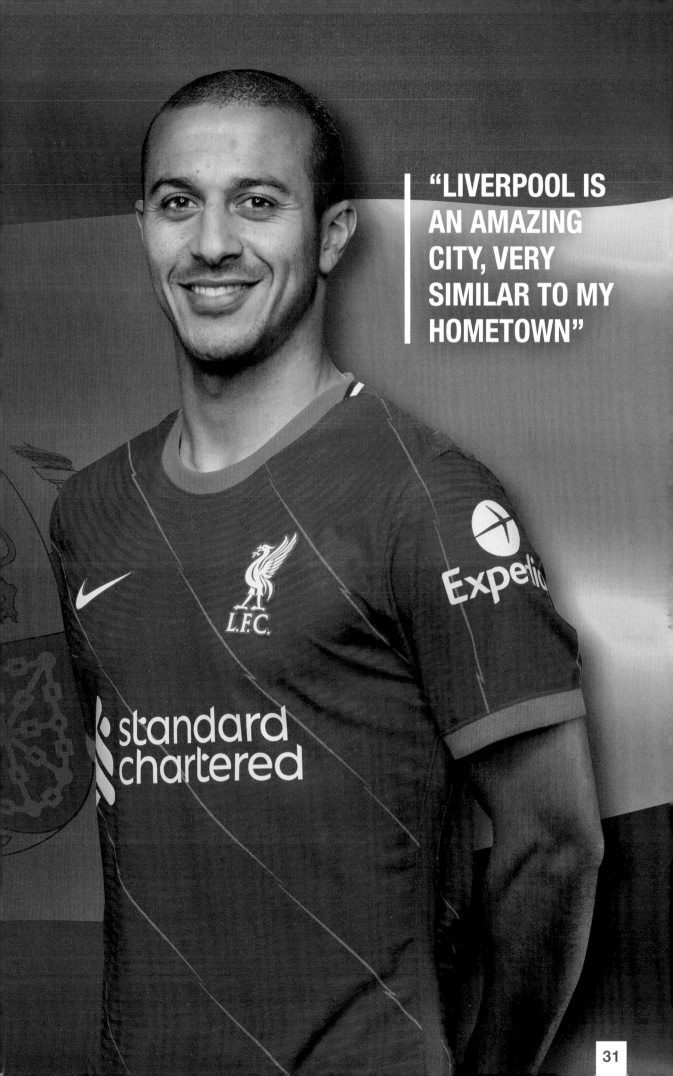

"LIVERPOOL IS AN AMAZING CITY, VERY SIMILAR TO MY HOMETOWN"

"I HAVE MASSIVE RESPECT FOR THE STORY OF STEVEN GERRARD IN THIS CLUB, HE CHANGED THE CLUB AS WELL"

Who would play alongside you in your dream five-a-side team?

Wow. I always say that, more than the best players, I will always choose the best chemistry and the best friends I have in football, like my brother Rafinha; Rodrigo Moreno, who plays in Leeds; Jonathan dos Santos, who's with LA Galaxy in the USA; David de Gea, goalkeeper for Man U; and myself - I think that's the five-a-side I would choose. The only problem is, somebody has to defend, but it's OK!

Have you tried a dish of Scouse yet?

Now when we have time with the family, my children love to be in the kitchen with us and try to do new dishes, so why not? I've learned a dish from Munich, and also I will learn a Scouse dish, 100 per cent.

What about the Thiago song…

Yeah, for me it's unbelievable! I guess surprised, I was surprised how fast…It's very funny, the video is amazing. How fast the people could, first of all, create the lyric, and second, the pictures, the video. It was very fast, I remember I was flying from Munich to get to Liverpool, and I saw the video and said,"Wow, I didn't even land here and I have this!" So, yeah, looking forward to when the stadium is full with people again and we can hear that song as well, for sure.

How much are you looking forward to seeing a full Anfield chanting your name?

First of all, I want to hear a goal from Liverpool, first of all I want to hear the famous chanting of Liverpool fans, and then, if things are going good, the play, they like me and I like them for sure, then I would love to hear that, but first of all let's hear the Liverpool songs and when we score also, that emotion with the fans. For me, that's more important than a personal one.

Which retired midfielder would you have loved to have played alongside?

I have already played with Xabi Alonso, and I can tick this box and say, "OK, I've played with him." And why not with Steven Gerrard, a legend? He was a midfield player. If I played alongside him, for me it would be a way to learn more football!

Favourite movie or TV series of all-time?

I would say some classical thing like Gladiator. The night before a game you try to get motivated with it, and comedies, actions… I don't know, it depends on your mood on the day, but I think great movies. I was a big fan of Breaking Bad, Friends as well, it's a classic one, amazing. Entourage, when I was 18 I started to watch it, and it was pretty funny as well.

What was the first football kit you ever had and did you have a name on the back?

My first kit was from the team of my dad, which was Valencia. We had it there in Spain, I remember perfectly wearing that kit and we didn't want to take it off to sleep - it was amazing.

Can you pick one of your tattoos and explain its meaning?

Yeah, for sure, it's very personal but in the end it's very public because we wear football shirts and they are short-sleeved. The most significant one is the picture of me: I was one year old and for me it means the football passion that I had since I was a kid, since I was a baby. I had that picture from my whole life, and it means a lot for me.

Is it acceptable to have pineapple on pizza?

Erm…It's acceptable to have everything in a dish, but for me, no. I don't like pineapple on pizza, and I'm the guy that loves to mix sweet and salty things.

Who is the funniest team-mate in the squad?

100 per cent Robbo - Andy Robertson. He's a very funny guy, a very natural person, everyone loves him and I think he's a great teammate.

What is your favourite Beatles song?

Wow…Hey Jude I think was the best I heard from The Beatles, first of all because my dad used to listen to a lot of these songs as well, English music. Also it reminds me a lot of football, because when I was young Hey Jude was on the channel before the football programme started, and I always linked this song with football, I don't know why. "Nah, nah-nah, nah-nah-nah-nah…" That one is a great one, yeah. Amazing.

3

FABINHO

MIDFIELDER

34

6

THIAGO
ALCÁNTARA

MIDFIELDER

YOUNG GUNS YOUTH CUP HEARTACHE

Liverpool's promising youngsters suffered a heart-breaking climax to the 2020/21 season, but it was another progressive campaign that everyone at the Academy can look back on with immense pride.

Following a commendable third place finish in the Premier League Under-18s North group, the young Reds fell at the final hurdle in the FA Youth Cup.

Led by coach Marc Bridge-Wilkinson, they were aiming to put Liverpool's name on the prestigious trophy for a fifth time and had battled through five rounds to reach the final.

It was a run that included outstanding away wins against Manchester United and Leicester, a quarter-final victory at home to Arsenal and a semi-final in which they had to come from behind to beat Ipswich at Portman Road.

In what was the club's eighth Youth Cup final appearance they again had to travel, this time to Villa Park to face a strong Aston Villa side, and it was the hosts who raced into an early two-goal lead.

Although the Kop kids later rallied and managed to pull a goal back, it wasn't enough to bring the silverware home but, despite the obvious disappointment, that shouldn't detract from what was a memorable journey.

"We're really proud of them. It's been a good, positive season," said Bridge-Wilkinson. "We can take great pride in the fact that we got here. The boys have shown an awful lot of potential. This is the first competitive final that some of them will have played and it's a learning curve."

FA Youth Cup run 2020/21

Round	Opposition	Result	Scorers
3rd rd:	Sutton United (h)	6-0	Musialowski 2, Morton, Ennis 3
4th rd:	Manchester United (a)	1-0	Morton
5th rd:	Leicester City (a)	5-1	Balagizi 3, Woltman 2
Q-final:	Arsenal (h)	3-1	Musialowski, Norris, Woltman
S-final:	Ipswich Town (a)	2-1	Musialowski, Frauendorf
Final:	Aston Villa (a)	1-2	Raven (OG)

Liverpool's 2020/21 FA Youth Cup squad (appearances in brackets)

Harvey Davies (6)
James Norris (6)
Jarell Quansah (6)
Luca Stephenson (6)
Dominic Corness (6)
Tyler Morton (6)
Max Woltman (6)

James Balagizi (6)
Mateusz Musialowski (6)
Conor Bradley (5)
Billy Koumetio (5)
Melkamu Frauendorf (4)
Isaac Mabaya (2)
Lee Jonas (2)

Fabian Mrozek (1)
Sean Wilson (1)
Luke Chambers (1)
Ethan Ennis (1)
Tommy Pilling (1)
James McConnell (1)

Unused subs: Stefan Bajcetic, Charlie Hayes-Green, Oscar Kelly

Hendo MBE

Jordan Henderson's status as a legendary footballer has long been assured, but it's not just his heroic deeds on the pitch that have earned him widespread praise and a multitude of honours.

The Liverpool captain is also a tireless worker for charity and has been an actively influential figure throughout the coronavirus pandemic.

An architect of the 'Players Together' initiative that encouraged professional footballers to donate to the NHS, he subsequently became an ambassador for the NHS Charities Together organisation and has also supported Cybersmile's anti-cyberbullying campaign 'People Not Profiles'.

In recognition of all this, Henderson became the proud recipient of an MBE in June 2021.

A richly deserved award for a great footballer and even better human being.

in the knowledge I was part of something special, rather than the reason for it.

"The other Premier League captains were the catalyst and the rest of the players, including my own teammates at Liverpool, were a driving force behind the scenes. Huge numbers of football fans from across the country also displayed great generosity in donating.

"But the true heroes are the NHS staff; they put themselves in harm's way to serve and protect us.

"Therefore I dedicate this to all the nurses, doctors, carers, porters, admin workers, cleaners, security personnel and every single individual who devotes their career and their lives to making the NHS the part of British life we are rightly most proud of as a nation."

HENDO SAYS...

"My family and I feel greatly humbled to be recognised in this way, more so given the reason for it.

"There are many privileges that come from playing professional football but having a platform to promote a charitable cause such as Players Together and NHS Charities Together is as big a privilege as any.

"It's important for me to state that although the honour has been issued to me personally, the credit must be shared to a far larger group of people and I accept this

> "THE TRUE HEROES ARE THE NHS STAFF; THEY PUT THEMSELVES IN HARM'S WAY TO SERVE AND PROTECT US"
>
> **Jordan Henderson**

APPEARANCES

Name	League	FA Cup	League Cup	Europe	Other	Total
Georginio Wijnaldum	38	2	1	9	1	51
Mohamed Salah	37	2	1	10	1	51
Andy Robertson	38	1	0	10	1	50
Sadio Mané	35	2	0	10	1	48
Roberto Firmino	36	2	0	9	1	48
Trent Alexander-Arnold	36	1	0	8	0	45
Fabinho Tavares	30	2	1	8	1	42
Alisson Becker	33	1	0	7	1	42
James Milner	26	2	1	6	1	36
Curtis Jones	24	2	2	5	1	34
Diogo Jota	19	0	2	9	0	30
Thiago Alcântara	24	2	0	4	0	30
Jordan Henderson	21	1	0	6	0	28
Xherdan Shaqiri	14	2	1	5	0	22
Nathaniel Phillips	17	0	0	3	0	20
Rhys Williams	9	2	2	6	0	19
Takumi Minamino	9	1	2	4	1	17
Divock Origi	9	2	2	4	0	17
Alex Oxlade-Chamberlain	13	1	0	3	0	17
Naby Keita	10	0	1	4	1	16
Neco Williams	6	1	2	4	1	14
Ozan Kabak	9	0	0	4	0	14
Joël Matip	10	0	0	2	0	12
Joe Gomez	7	0	1	3	1	12
Virgil Van Dijk	5	0	2	0	1	8
Kostas Tsimikas	2	0	1	4	0	7
Adrian San Miguel	3	0	2	1	0	6
Caoimhin Kelleher	2	1	0	2	0	5
Marko Grujic	0	0	2	0	0	2
Harry Wilson	0	0	1	0	0	1
Rhian Brewster	0	0	0	0	1	1
Harvey Elliott	0	0	1	0	0	1
Leighton Clarkson	0	0	0	1	0	1
Billy Koumetio	0	0	0	1	0	1

Roberto **Firmino** made the most assists (9)

TEAM STATS

Total games:	53	Average attendance at home - league:	842
Games won:	28	Average attendance at home - overall:	666
Games drawn:	13	Average goals per game - League:	1.53
Games lost:	12	Average goals per game - Overall:	1.33
Clean sheets - league:	12	Average goal minute - League:	53
Clean sheets - overall:	20	Average goal minute - Overall:	51
Total goals:	97		

WE SCORED **97** GOALS!

38

GOALS

Name	League	FA Cup	League Cup	Europe	Other	Total
Mohamed Salah	22	3	0	6	0	31
Sadio Mané	11	2	0	3	0	16
Diogo Jota	9	0	0	4	0	13
Roberto Firmino	9	0	0	0	0	9
Own goals	3	0	0	1	0	4
Curtis Jones	1	0	2	1	0	4
Takumi Minamino	1	0	2	0	1	4
Georginio Wijnaldum	2	1	0	0	0	3
Trent Alexander-Arnold	2	0	0	0	0	2
Joël Matip	1	0	0	0	0	1
Jordan Henderson	1	0	0	0	0	1
Divock Origi	0	0	1	0	0	1
Marko Grujic	0	0	1	0	0	1
Xherdan Shaqiri	0	0	1	0	0	1
Alisson Becker	1	0	0	0	0	1
Nathaniel Phillips	1	0	0	0	0	1
Andy Robertson	1	0	0	0	0	1
Alex Oxlade-Chamberlain	1	0	0	0	0	1
Virgil Van Dijk	1	0	0	0	0	1
Thiago Alcântara	1	0	0	0	0	1

GOAL MINUTES

Goals from 1 to 15:	9
Goals from 16 to 30:	8
Goals from 31 to 45:	21
Goals from 46 to 60:	23
Goals from 61 to 75:	18
Goals from 76 to 90:	18
Goals from 91 to 120:	0

GOALS SPLIT DOWN TO COMPETITIONS

Premier League	68	FA Cup	6
Champions League	15	Community Shield	1
League Cup	7		

TOP 5 PLAYERS WITH MOST ASSISTS

Name	League	FA Cup	League Cup	Europe	Other	Total
Roberto Firmino	7	2	0	0	0	9
Trent Alexander-Arnold	7	0	0	2	0	9
Sadio Mané	7	0	0	1	0	8
Andy Robertson	7	0	0	0	0	7
Mohamed Salah	5	0	0	1	0	6

CLEAN SHEETS

Name	League	FA Cup	League Cup	Europe	Other	Total

INDIVIDUAL AWARDS

LFC STANDARD CHARTERED PLAYER OF THE SEASON

1. Mohamed Salah
2. Fabinho Tavarez
3. Nathaniel Phillips

> Mohamed **Salah**

OF COURSE, I'M HAPPY TO WIN THIS AWARD, ESPECIALLY AS IT IS VOTED FOR BY FANS, BUT WINNING OUR FINAL GAMES AND QUALIFYING FOR THE CHAMPIONS LEAGUE WAS THE MOST IMPORTANT THING. I THINK I HAVE PLAYED OK THIS SEASON, BUT IT'S NOT ABOUT ME – IT'S ABOUT THE TEAM. FOR US AS A TEAM, I THINK IF WE'D HAD THE FANS IN THE STADIUM, OUR POSITION, OUR SITUATION, WOULD HAVE BEEN MUCH BETTER. WE SUFFERED A LOT THIS SEASON WITH MISSING THE FANS. SO I AM HAPPY IN THE LAST GAME OF THE SEASON WE PLAYED WITH OUR FANS. IT WAS GREAT TO SEE THEM BACK IN THE STADIUM. I WANT TO SAY THANK YOU VERY MUCH FOR VOTING FOR ME, I'M VERY PROUD ABOUT THAT.

LFC STANDARD CHARTERED PLAYER OF THE MONTH

September	Sadio Mané
October	Diogo Jota
November	Diogo Jota
December	Mohamed Salah
January	Mohamed Salah
February	Mohamed Salah
March	Nathanial Phillips
April	Trent Alexander-Arnold

PREMIER LEAGUE MANAGER OF THE MONTH

May	Jürgen Klopp

PREMIER LEAGUE GOAL OF THE MONTH

YOU'LL NEVER WALK ALONE

LIVERPOOL
FOOTBALL CLUB

EST·1892

C

14

JORDAN

HENDERSON

MIDFIELDER

17

CURTIS JONES

MIDFIELDER

Matt BEARD

Matt Beard has his sights set on re-establishing Liverpool as a major force in the Women's game once again. And there are few people more qualified to rekindle those past glory days than the 43-year-old Londoner.

New boss Beard was previously in charge of the Reds between 2012 and 2015 - a halcyon era in the team's history.

During this period, he masterminded back-to-back title triumphs in the Women's Super League (2013 and 2014) and then took them into the Champions League for the first time.

He has since worked in America, with Boston Breakers, and managed West Ham United Women and, more recently, Bristol City Women.

In April 2021, six years after his first stint as manager came to an end, his return to Liverpool was announced.

"When the opportunity arose it was something I wanted to do. I've always followed the club since I left, it's close to my heart," he says.

"When you're here and then you're away from the football club you realise how special and unique it is.

"I've never been in a city or worked for a football club where the football is the be all and end all to the supporters. It's a fascinating football club, it's a fascinating city."

Having missed out on promotion from the FA Women's Championship last season, Beard's first challenge in his second spell at the club is to restore Liverpool's top-flight status.

"My memories from before are great memories and will always be with me," he adds. "But it's about what I do this time and hopefully getting the club back into the Super League.

"One thing I can promise the football club and the fans is that I'll work as hard as I can to get us back there."

LIVERPOOL FC WOMEN: HISTORIC TIMELINE

1989 Formed as Newton Ladies FC
1991 Changed name to Knowsley United WFC
1994 FA Women's Cup runners-up
1994 Association with LFC made official and name changed to Liverpool Ladies FC
1995 FA Women's Cup runners-up
1996 FA Women's Cup runners-up
2004 FA Women's Premier League Northern Division champions

2007 FA Women's Premier League Northern Division champions
2010 FA Women's Premier League Northern Division champions
2011 Founding members of the FA Women's Super League
2013 FA Women's Super League champions
2014 FA Women's Super League champions
2018 Club rebranded and became known as Liverpool FC Women

INTRODUCING
Missy Bo KEARNS

Talented, popular and Scouse, Missy Bo Kearns is a rising star who is living the dream with Liverpool FC Women.

Raised in Allerton and a dyed-in-the-wool Liverpudlian, Kearns first pulled on the red shirt at under-11 level, shortly before she turned nine, and has worked her way impressively through the youth ranks at the club.

In 2018/19 she was part of the development squad that clinched a league and cup double, while international recognition also came her way in the form of a call-up to the England under-17 and under-19 sides.

Kearns' eye-catching performances in midfield not surprisingly saw her called up to the first team and in 2020/21, following a brief loan spell at Blackburn, she firmly established herself in the side, making 20 appearances and scoring two goals.

The fine form shown by Kearns prompted the club to offer her a first professional contract in January 2021.

PROFILE

Birthplace:	Liverpool
Date of birth:	14 April 2001
Position:	Midfield
Squad number:	7

Come the end of that season she was the deserving recipient of the Liverpool FC Women's Player of the Year accolade and also scooped the fans' award.

Now aged 20, Kearns reinforced her commitment to the Reds when signing a new contract in the summer of 2021 and a bright future beckons for our number seven.

"IT'S A DREAM COME TRUE TO CONTINUE STAYING AT THE CLUB, IT'S A BIG HONOUR FOR ME. I JUST WANT TO PLAY FOR LIVERPOOL AND I'M OVER THE MOON. INDIVIDUALLY, LAST YEAR WAS MY BREAKTHROUGH SEASON. I GOT THE OPPORTUNITY JUST AFTER CHRISTMAS TO SHOWCASE WHAT I CAN DO AND I FEEL I TOOK THAT CHANCE. IT STILL FEELS LIKE YESTERDAY I WAS IN THE U11S AND I'VE TAKEN IT ALL DAY BY DAY AND JUST ENJOYED EACH MOMENT PLAYING WITH A LIVERPOOL SHIRT ON." Missy Bo Kearns

RED-UCATION

Welcome to home-schooling LFC-style! Use your LFC knowledge to test yourself in a variety of subjects. Warning: some revision may be required!

A ENGLISH

1. List five adjectives to describe Liverpool's Champions League victory over Barcelona in 2019...

....

2. Which former Liverpool manager once said, "There are two teams on Merseyside: Liverpool and Liverpool reserves"?

....

3. There are six incorrect facts in this statement? Circle those that you spot...

Liverpool Football Club was formed in 1901 and originally they played in blue and white shirts. Their home ground is Old Trafford and they are the most successful team in English football. Club legends include 'King' Kevin Dalglish and former goalkeeper Steven Gerrard. The current club captain is Jordan Henderson and in 2019 he lifted the Champions League trophy at Wembley after Liverpool defeated Tottenham. The following year Liverpool became champions of England for the 18th time.

4. Fill in the blank...

At his first press conference as Liverpool manager, Jürgen Klopp described himself as the '............... one'.

5. Complete the following sentence: Liverpool Football Club is the best in the world because

....

HISTORY

1. Who founded Liverpool Football Club?..
2. In what year did Bill Shankly become Liverpool manager?...................
3. What club did Liverpool defeat to win the European Cup for the first time in 1977?...................
4. Which competition did Liverpool win on four successive occasions in the 1980s?...................
5. By what score did Liverpool beat Alaves to complete a cup treble in 2001?...................

GEOGRAPHY

1. Liverpool's home ground is in Anfield but in what area of Merseyside is the club's training ground?...................
2. Name the Italian city where Liverpool have twice lifted the European Cup?...................
3. In which country did Liverpool become world champions in December 2019?...................
4. Where in Australia did Liverpool attract a crowd of over 95,000 for a friendly in July 2013?...................
5. In which one of the following continents are Liverpool yet to play a match: Africa, Asia or South America?

MATHS

ANSWERS ARE ON PAGE 61

1. In total, how many European trophies have Liverpool won?...............
2. Is Anfield's record attendance closer to 50,000, 60,000 or 70,000?...............
3. If you took away his penalties, how many goals did Mo Salah score for Liverpool in 2020/21?...............
4. How many years separated Liverpool's first and second FA Cup triumphs?...............
5. If you made 40 appearances per season how many seasons would it take for you to overtake the club's current all-time record appearance holder Ian Callaghan, who made 857? ....

 # FOREIGN LANGUAGES

"Hello and welcome to the six-time European champions"

Can you translate the phrase above into the native language of the Liverpool manager and four of his players?

Jürgen Klopp...

Thiago...

Diogo Jota..

Virgil van Dijk..

Ibrahimha Konaté...

ART

Here are some famous Liverpool banners. Can you design your own on a spare piece of paper?

20

DIOGO JOTA

FORWARD

ROBERTO FIRMINO

9

FORWARD

47

A-to-Z
of LFC

Ambitious, bold, celebrated, distinctive, eminent, famous, glorious, historic, incredible, joyous, kindred, legendary, magical, nostalgic, outstanding, passionate, quality, respected, successful, triumphant, unique, victorious, wonderful, x-factor, yours, zealous.

Our alphabetical guide to Liverpool Football Club…

A is for...

- Our home ground **Anfield**
- Spanish midfield maestro Xabi **Alonso**
- Late 80s goal-poacher John **Aldridge**

Can you think of more?

B is for...

- Former wing wizard John **Barnes**
- 2005 Champions League-winning manager Rafael **Benitez**
- The legendary **Bootroom**

Can you think of more?

C is for...

- Club record appearance holder Ian **Callaghan**
- **Campione** Liverpool!
- **'Corner** taken quickly' - now an immortal line of commentary

Can you think of more?

D is for...

- King Kenny **Dalglish**
- **Derby** games against our rivals across Stanley Park
- The big Pole in our goal from 2005, Jerzy **Dudek**

Can you think of more?

E is for...

- Former player, coach and manager Roy **Evans**
- **Europe**, a continent we have conquered six times
- Promising youngster Harvey **Elliott**

Can you think of more?

F

is for...

- The original treble-winning manager Joe **Fagan**
- **FA** Cup, first won in 1965 and now we have seven of them
- David **Fairclough**, football's most famous supersub

Can you think
of more?

G

is for...

- **Goals** - what we all love to see
- Steven **Gerrard**, captain fantastic from 2003 to 2015
- **God**, aka Robbie Fowler

Can you think
of more?

H

is for...

- Club captain Jordan **Henderson**
- Goalscoring legend of the 1960s, Roger **Hunt**
- 1986 Double-winning skipper Alan **Hansen**

Can you think
of more?

I

is for...

- The miracle of **Istanbul**
- Anfield **Iron**, nickname of former captain Tommy Smith
- **Injury** time goals, like Alisson's v West Brom

Can you think
of more?

J

is for...

- '**Joey** Ate The Frogs Legs' - our most famous banner
- **Justice** for the 97
- Portuguese forward Diogo **Jota**

Can you think
of more?

K

is for...

- Anfield's world-renowned former terrace, the Spion **Kop**
- Jürgen **Klopp**, our talismanic leader since 2015
- Seventies superstar Kevin **Keegan**

Can you think
of more?

L

is for...

- 19 **League** titles
- Legendary player Billy **Liddell**
- **Liverbird**, the proud emblem of our club

Can you think
of more?

Can you think
of more?

N **is for...**

- Phil **Neal**, the club's most decorated player
- Unsung hero of the great 1980s team, Steve **Nicol**
- '**Never** Give Up' - a slogan forever associated with the Champions League comeback against Barcelona in 2019

Can you think
of more?

O **is for...**

- Michael **Owen**, hero of our 2001 FA Cup win
- **Orange**, the colour of Liverpool's third kit in 2017/18
- Cult striker Divock **Origi**, scorer of iconic goals

Can you think
of more?

P **is for...**

- The most successful English manager of all-time, Bob **Paisley**
- **Poor** Scouser Tommy, a popular song sung on the Kop
- **Parc** Des Princes, venue for the 1981 European Cup final

Can you think
of more?

Q **is for...**

- **Quickest** ever LFC goal, scored by Paul Walsh in 1984
- **Quiet** - something that can never be used to describe Anfield!
- Champions League **qualification**, the minimum requirement for LFC each season

Can you think
of more?

R **is for...**

- Master marksman Ian **Rush**, the club's all-time record goalscorer
- **Rome**, Italian city where Liverpool have twice lifted the European Cup
- **Red**, the colour of Liverpool's home shirt since 1896

Can you think
of more?

S **is for...**

- Bill **Shankly**, the club's most iconic former manager
- Egyptian goal king Mo **Salah**
- **Supporters**: Liverpool's 12th man

Can you think
of more?

T is for...

- Trophies - we currently have 42 in total and want more
- The famous 'This Is Anfield' sign
- Team of Macs - nickname of the club's first ever side

Can you think
of more?

U is for...

- UEFA Cup, a competition we've won three times
- The 68-game unbeaten home run between April 2017 and January 2021
- Uruguay, country where there is another team called Liverpool

Can you think
of more?

V is for...

- Our centre half and number four, Virgil van Dijk
- Victory - the sweet taste of which we can't get enough of
- Barry Venison, full-back signed from Sunderland in 1986

Can you think
of more?

W is for...

- World Champions: a feat finally achieved in Doha 2019
- Ronnie Whelan, former captain and scorer of spectacular goals
- Wembley, the scene of countless memorable moments

Can you think
of more?

X is for...

- Abel Xavier, Portuguese defender signed from Everton in 2002
- Xmas Day, a date Liverpool haven't played a fixture on since 1957
- X-rated challenges, the likes of which we hopefully won't be seeing many of

Can you think
of more?

Y is for...

- LFC anthem 'You'll Never Walk Alone'
- Ron Yeats, the first Liverpool captain to lift the FA Cup
- FA Youth Cup, a tournament won four times

Can you think
of more?

Z is for...

- Zimbabwe, country with whom Bruce Grobbelaar made 32 international appearances
- Christian Ziege, German full-back who was part of the 2001 treble-winning squad
- Zagreb, birthplace of former midfielder Igor Biscan

Can you think
of more?

10

SADIO MANÉ

FORWARD

LIVERPOOL
FOOTBALL CLUB
YOU'LL NEVER WALK ALONE
EST·1892

11

MOHAMED SALAH

FORWARD

53

WELCOME TO LIVERPOOL

Ibrahima
KONATÉ

FACT FILE

Date of birth: **25 May 1999**

Birthplace: **Paris, France**

Height: **Six foot four inches**

Former clubs:
Sochaux (2014-17)
Red Bull Leipzig (2017-21)

Joined LFC: **July 2021**

5 Competitive Debut: **tbc**

Get to know more about Liverpool's newest centre-back…

You have chosen to wear the number five shirt. Is that a special number to you, is there a reason why you picked it?
No, I think it's an important number for this club. A great player had this number before me. I have not [much] pressure but a little bit of pressure because I have to improve for the future. I hope I will do great things with this number.

Fellow central defenders Virgil van Dijk, Joe Gomez and Joel Matip…are these players you hope you'll be able to learn from?
Yes, of course. Of course I will learn [from] these players, but not just with these players, with every player on this team. It's just the start and with time it will be [a lot] better.

At the pre-season training camp which players did you first bond with and have conversations with?
With van Dijk a little bit; Mané because he speaks French; Naby, I knew him for a long time; Origi and Salah. I think I can speak with every player step by step - it will be good. All of the team are good guys.

Tell us about the conversation with Jürgen Klopp. What has he asked you to do? What has he told you about the expectations for you this year?
We spoke before my signature, but this will stay between us. Yes, I know I am very young but this is not important – I have to improve on the pitch and to work. If I am good, for the rest it is not important.

You didn't play for Leipzig against Liverpool last season, but were you dreaming then that perhaps one day you could be a Liverpool player?
No, I think not – but, yes, I was very sad to not play against Liverpool because it is one of the best teams in the world and when you are a football player you like to play in these games. We lost and I could not help the team in this moment and I was sad, but now I am very happy because I am in this team. Yes, I am happy!

What can Liverpool fans expect to see from you? Can you describe your style to them?
Yes, I am big, I am strong and I am not scared with the ball! I can score more with my foot than my head, it is a little bit strange! This is me! Yes, I have this quality, but I have to work again and again and more and more and more for being a very good defender.

How excited are you about playing in the Premier League?
Of course, of course, of course. This is not a question!

You think you're suited to that style? The pace and intensity of the Premier League?
Yes, I have watched some Premier League games and everybody knows there is so much intensity, strong players. This is difficult but I [will] love the challenge.

The fans will want to know what to call you; is there a nickname you like to be called?
Yes, 'Ibou' because when I was young, every time my mother would call me 'Ibou, Ibou'. When I was on the first day in Leipzig, she was with me and she would say every time, 'Hey, Ibou… Ibou… Ibou…' and Ralf Rangnick asked, 'Why 'Ibou'?' So, I said it was my nickname because every time my mum would call me that every time and my family too. He said, 'OK, now it's Ibou' and afterwards everyone would call me it.

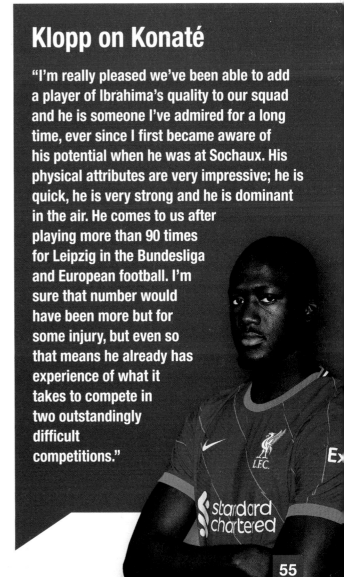

Klopp on Konaté

"I'm really pleased we've been able to add a player of Ibrahima's quality to our squad and he is someone I've admired for a long time, ever since I first became aware of his potential when he was at Sochaux. His physical attributes are very impressive; he is quick, he is very strong and he is dominant in the air. He comes to us after playing more than 90 times for Leipzig in the Bundesliga and European football. I'm sure that number would have been more but for some injury, but even so that means he already has experience of what it takes to compete in two outstandingly difficult competitions."

130 Years of LFC

To commemorate the club's forthcoming 130th birthday in 2022, here are some standout facts & figures from the past 13 decades…

8 LEAGUE CUPS

6 EUROPEAN CUP/ CHAMPIONS LEAGUE TROPHIES

5,795 competitive fixtures played

857 appearances by Ian Callaghan*

10,072 goals scored by Liverpool in all competitive fixtures

3 UEFA Cups

472 games in which Steven Gerrard captained the Reds*

1 – FIFA Club World Cup

17 HAT-TRICKS REGISTERED BY GORDON HODGSON*

417 consecutive appearances by **PHIL NEAL***

a history in numbers

*denotes a club record

323
CLEAN SHEETS

kept by **Ray Clemence***

19
TIMES CHAMPIONS OF ENGLAND

20 – different full-time managers

4 UEFA SUPER CUPS

777 players to have represented the first team in a competitive match

18 goals netted by Supersub David Fairclough when coming off the bench*

460 different Liverpool goalscorers

7 FA Cups

346 GOALS scored by Ian Rush*

61,905
Anfield's record attendance, set in February 1952

11 GOALS scored without reply in the club's record victory v Stromsgodet in 1974*

*(all stats correct prior to the start of the 2021/22 season)

THIS IS ANFIELD

HENDERSON 14

WE ARE L

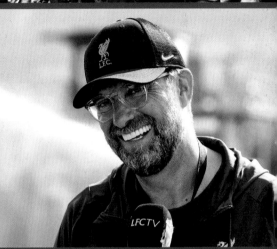

VERPOOL

2021/22 FIXTURE TRACKER

*All fixtures subject to change

 **PREMIER LEAGUE**

2021

August

14	Norwich City	(A)
21	Burnley	(H)
28	Chelsea	(H)

September

12	Leeds United	(A)
18	Crystal Palace	(H)
25	Brentford	(A)

October

2	Manchester City	(H)
16	Watford	(A)
23	Manchester United	(A)
30	Brighton & Hove Albion	(H)

November

6	West Ham United	(A)
20	Arsenal	(H)
27	Southampton	(H)
30	Everton	(A)

December

4	Wolverhampton Wanderers	(A)
11	Aston Villa	(H)
15	Newcastle United	(H)
18	Tottenham Hotspur	(A)
26	Leeds United	(H)
28	Leicester City	(A)

2022

January

1	Chelsea	(A)
15	Brentford	(H)
22	Crystal Palace	(A)

February

9	Leicester City	(H)
12	Burnley	(A)
19	Norwich City	(H)
26	Arsenal	(A)

March

5	West Ham United	(H)
12	Brighton & Hove Albion	(A)
19	Manchester United	(H)

April

2	Watford	(H)
9	Manchester City	(A)
16	Aston Villa	(A)
23	Everton	(H)
30	Newcastle United	(A)

May

7	Tottenham Hotspur	(H)
15	Southampton	(A)
22	Wolverhampton Wanderers	(H)

 FA CUP

January 8	3rd round	V		H/A	
February 5	4th round	V		H/A	
March 2	5th round	V		H/A	
March 19	Quarter-final	V		H/A	
April 16	Semi-final	V		N	
May 14	FINAL	V		N	

 LEAGUE CUP

September 22	3rd round	V		H/A	
October 27	4th round	V		H/A	
December 22	5th round	V		H/A	
January 5	Semi-final 1st leg	V		H/A	
January 12	Semi-final 2nd leg	V		H/A	
February 27	FINAL	V		N	

CHAMPIONS LEAGUE

*MD = Matchday

August					
15	MD1	V	H/A		
22	MD2	V	H/A		

October					
20	MD3	V	H/A		

November					
3	MD4	V	H/A		
24	MD5	V	H/A		

December					
8	MD6	V	H/A		

February					
16/23	Last 16 1st leg	V	H/A		

March					
9/16	Last 16 2nd leg	V	H/A		

April					
6	Quarter-final 1st leg	V	H/A		
13	Quarter-final 2nd leg	V	H/A		
27	Semi-final 1st leg	V	H/A		

May					
4	Semi-final 2nd leg	V	H/A		
28	FINAL	V	N		

THE QUIZ ANSWERS!

RED-UCATION (P.44)

A ENGLISH

1. n/a personal preference
2. Bill Shankly
3. Liverpool Football Club was formed in (1901) and originally the played in blue and white shirts. Their home ground is (Old Trafford) and they are the most successful team in English football. Club legends include 'King' (Kevin) Dalglish and former (goalkeeper) Steven Gerrard. The current club captain is Jordan Henderson and in 2019 he lifted the Champions League trophy at (Wembley) after Liverpool defeated Tottenham. The following year Liverpool became champions of England for the (18th) time.
4. Normal
5. n/a personal preference

WORDSEARCH (P.27)

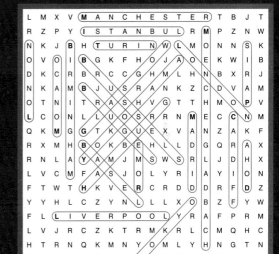

HISTORY

1. John Houlding
2. 1959
3. Borussia Moenchengladbach
4. League Cup
5. 5-4

GEOGRAPHY

1. Kirkby
2. Rome
3. Qatar
4. Melbourne
5. South America

MATHS

1. 13
2. 60,000
3. 24
4. Nine
5. 22

You're Boss! Well done.

FOREIGN LANGUAGES

1. Hallo und willkommen beim sechsfachen Europameister
2. Hola y bienvenido a los seis veces campeones de Europa
3. Olá e bem-vindos aos seis vezes campeões europeus
4. Hallo en welkom bij de zesvoudig Europees kampioen
5. Bonjour et bienvenue aux sextuples champions d'Europe